Hide and Sleep

Happy House

About Wise & Wide

- A systematic 6-level English reading program based on Lexile® measures
- Diverse and interesting topics chosen from the elementary curriculums of Korea and English speaking western countries
- Well-written books in various forms including fiction stories, descriptive texts, and classics retold
- The informative but original fiction stories grab your interest, leading to the easy and clear understanding of the educational content.
- Improve thinking skills with solid after-reading activities at all levels of the series.

Wise & Wide is a 6-level English reading program that consists of 60 books and each level is systematically divided by Lexile® measures. The Lexile® Framework for Reading is the most popular reading measuring system in American formal education curriculums and many English programs. Over 20 out of 50 states in the U.S. mark Lexile® measures directly on students' final report cards and over 300 well-known publishers adopt and use Lexile® measures.

Experience many kinds of readings written by professional writers from the U.S. and England. They used interesting topics that were carefully chosen after analyzing elementary curriculums from around the world including Korea, the U.S., England, and Australia among many others. Comprehensive after-reading activities including graphic organizers, speaking tasks, and After-reading Tests are ready for you.

Levels in the series and their corresponding Lexile® measures

Level	Lexile® measures	U.S. Grade
Level 1	Below 200L	Pre K - K
Level 2	190L - 400L	Lower Grade 1
Level 3	350L - 530L	Upper Grade 1
Level 4	420L - 650L	Grade 2
Level 5	520L - 940L	Grade 3 - 4
Level 6	830L - 1070L	Grade 5 - 6

* Smart Readers: Wise & Wide level 1 is applicable to the preschool level in the U.S.

* The source of the relationship between Lexile® measures and U.S. school grades: CCSS(Common Core State Standards) FOR ENGLISH LANGUAGE ARTS, APPENDIX A (2012, which is used by 45 states in the U.S.)

Topic List

	Level 1	Level 2	Level 3	Level 4	Level 5	Level 6
Book 1	Science>Biology: The hibernation of animals Story	Science>Biology: Living and nonliving things Story	Science>Biology> Animals & the Environment: Sea otters Story	Environment> Living with nature: The diver & the persimmon tree Story	Science>Biology> Animal: Amazing animals of the Amazon Story	Science>Biology: Germs, transmitted diseases Story
Book 2	Literature> World classics: Aesop's fables Story	Literature> Traditional fairy tale: Old tales about stones Story	Social Studies> Economy: To run a business to make and save money Story	Science>Biology> Plants: Photosynthesis Story	Science>Earth science: Earth's layers, earthquakes, volcanoes, and earth's atmosphere Report	Mathematics> Sequence: The golden ratio & the Fibonacci sequence Story
Book 3	Science>Physics: How shadows are formed Story	Literature> World classics: Peter Pan Story	Science>Scientific technology: Nanobots Story	Literature>Myths: World's creation stories Story	Literature> Legend: The story of King Arthur Story	Literature>Myths: Constellation myths Story
Book 4	Literature> Traditional literature: The Talmud Story	Science>Biology> Animal: Polar bears Story	Science>Biology> Animal: Mountain gorillas Story	Social Studies> Cultural anthropology: Amazing ancient cultures of the world Story	Science> Earth science: Clouds and weather Story	Literature> Human & animals: The friendship between a girl and a horse Story
Book 5	Social Studies> Ethics: Rules in daily life Story	Science>Biology: The five senses Report	Social Studies> Cultural anthropology: Astonishing festivals Report	Art>Music: Stories from two operas Story	Social Studies> World culture & history: The Renaissance Story	Sports> Board sports: Surfing & snowboarding Story
Book 6	Social Studies> World geography & travel: Tourist attractions around the world Story	Science>Biology> Animal: Dinosaurs Story	Science> Astronomy: The solar system Story	Social Studies> People: Three great people who overcame hardships Story	Science>Scientific technology: The wonderful world of robots Report	Art>Music: Composers of the Romantic Era Report
Book 7	Science> Space science: The life of astronauts Report	Social Studies> Cultural anthropology: Mythological monsters from around the world Report	Mathematics> Elementary mathematics: Numbers, measurement, shapes and data Report	Science & Social Studies> Technology & culture: Inventions from around the world Report	Art>Works of art: Famous paintings Report	Social Studies> Human & animals: Animals in action for human Report
Book 8	Social Studies> Cultural anthropology: Various living cultures of the world Story	Art>Music: Instruments in the orchestra Story	Social Studies> Life safety: Learning and using outdoor survival skills Story	Social Studies> History: The California Gold Rush Report	Social Studies & Science> Psychology: Psychology in everyday life Story	Literature> World classics: The Merchant of Venice Story
Book 9	Social Studies> Jobs: Interviews about jobs Report	Science>Scientific technology: Developments in technology in different times Story	Social Studies> Politics>Election: Running for 3rd grade class president Story	Literature> World classics: Stories of Sherlock Holmes Story	Literature> World classics: Adrift in the Pacific Story	Social Studies> History & People: Great world leaders in history Report
Book 10	Literature>Traditional fairy tale: Eastern and Western folk tales on the same theme Story	Sports>Winter sports: Various aspects of some Winter Olympic sports Report	Literature> World classics: Short stories by O. Henry Story	Sports> Ball games: Various aspects of popular ball games Report	Social Studies> History: Famous events that changed world history Report	Art & Social Studies> Art: Stories about the creation, distribution, and preservation of paintings Report

How to Use This Book

•Before Reading

You can easily find the topic and what kind of story you are about to read.

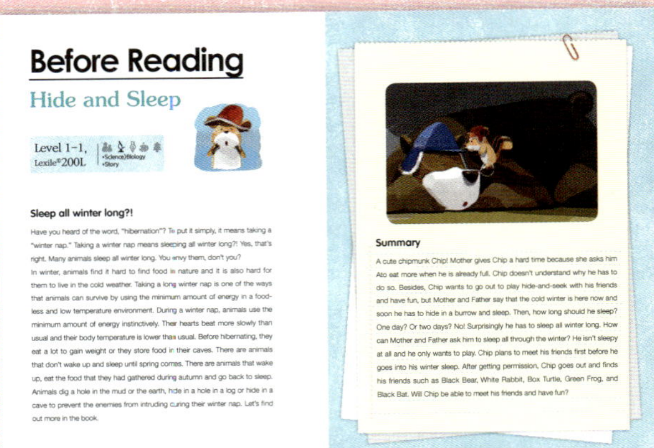

•The text

All the stories were written by professional writers from the U.S. and England, so you will read authentic and appropriate English sentences and expressions in every book in the series.

•Pop Quiz

Check out right away if you understand what you have just read by solving a pop quiz that checks your comprehension.

•Key Words

The key words and expressions on each page are listed for you to easily study them.

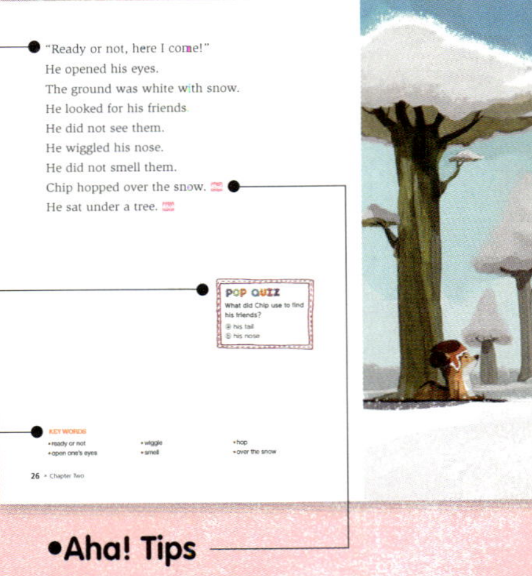

•Aha! Tips

Download free Korean explanations at *www.ihappyhouse.co.kr* for all of the sentences marked with "Aha!". These explain cultural, scientific, and economic knowledge or they deal with aspects of English such as grammatical structures or idiomatic expressions. There are lots of "Aha! Tips" to help you understand the text.

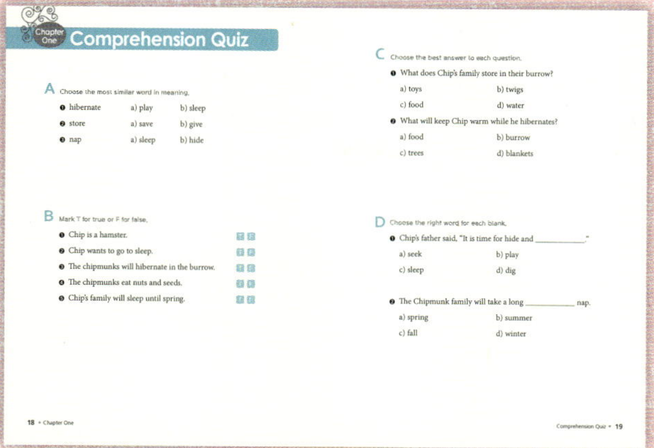

•Comprehension Quiz

After reading one chapter, solve various questions to find out if you fully understand the content.

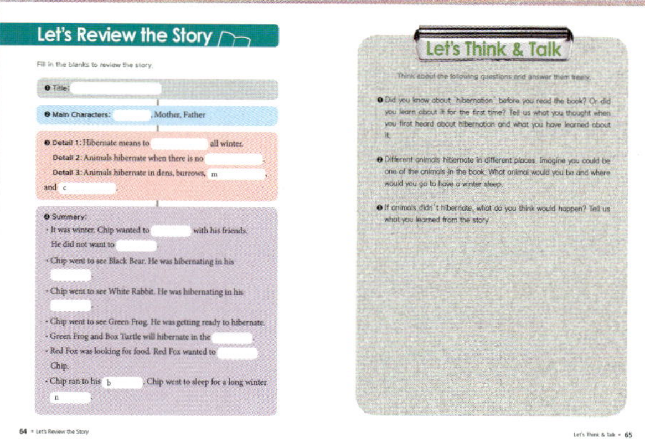

•Let's Review the Story /
•Let's Think & Talk

Fill in the blanks in the organizer to summarize the whole story. Express your own thinking and feelings about the story by answering the questions. You can build up logic and reasoning skills for your essay examinations in the future.

Appendix

Audio CD

In the CD audio book form, the texts are read vividly by American professional voice actors.
(MP3 files downloaded for free)

After-reading Test

Solve an additionally provided After-reading Test for each book.

The Korean translation, Answer Keys, a Word Quiz, a Word List, and Aha! Tips for each book

You can download them for free at *www.ihappyhouse.co.kr* or *www.darakwon.co.kr*

Before Reading

Hide and Sleep

Level 1–1,
Lexile® 200L

•Science〉Biology
•Story

Sleep all winter long?!

Have you heard of the word, "hibernation"? To put it simply, it means taking a "winter nap." Taking a winter nap means sleeping all winter long?! Yes, that's right. Many animals sleep all winter long. You envy them, don't you?

In winter, animals find it hard to find food in nature and it is also hard for them to live in the cold weather. Taking a long winter nap is one of the ways that animals can survive by using the minimum amount of energy in a food-less and low temperature environment. During a winter nap, animals use the minimum amount of energy instinctively. Their hearts beat more slowly than usual and their body temperature is lower than usual. Before hibernating, they eat a lot to gain weight or they store food in their caves. There are animals that don't wake up and sleep until spring comes. There are animals that wake up, eat the food that they had gathered during autumn and go back to sleep. Animals dig a hole in the mud or the earth, hide in a hole in a log or hide in a cave to prevent the enemies from intruding during their winter nap. Let's find out more in the book.

Summary

A cute chipmunk Chip! Mother gives Chip a hard time because she asks him to eat more when he is already full. Chip doesn't understand why he has to do so. Besides, Chip wants to go out to play hide-and-seek with his friends and have fun, but Mother and Father say that the cold winter is here now and soon he has to hide in a burrow and sleep. Then, how long should he sleep? One day? Or two days? No! Surprisingly he has to sleep all winter long. How can Mother and Father ask him to sleep all through the winter? He isn't sleepy at all and he only wants to play. Chip plans to meet his friends first before he goes into his winter sleep. After getting permission, Chip goes out and finds his friends such as Black Bear, White Rabbit, Box Turtle, Green Frog, and Black Bat. Will Chip be able to meet his friends and have fun?

Contents

Hide and Sleep

Hide and Sleep

Chip Wants to Play

"Eat your food, Chip.

Then we must sleep all winter."

Chip was a chipmunk.

His mother wanted him to eat.

She wanted him to eat and eat.

Chip did not want to eat.

Chip wanted to play.

"Why must I eat so much?"

Chip was full.

"We will not eat this winter."

Mother gave him a nut.

"We will take a long winter nap.

We will hide and sleep."

▲ chipmunk

Father said, "We will hibernate." 

"What does hibernate mean?"

Chip rubbed his head.

"It means to sleep all winter."

Mother gave Chip seeds.

"We hibernate in our burrow," Father added.

"Outside it will be cold.

There will be snow," Mother told Chip.

"Our burrow will keep us warm."

Mother patted a nest of grass and leaves.

KEY WORDS

- hibernate
- mean (mean-meant-meant)
- rub
- seed
- burrow
- add
- outside
- keep (keep-kept-kept)
- warm
- pat
- nest
- grass
- leaves
- hide-and-seek[hide and seek]
- paw
- shake one's head (shake-shook-shaken)
- it is not time for

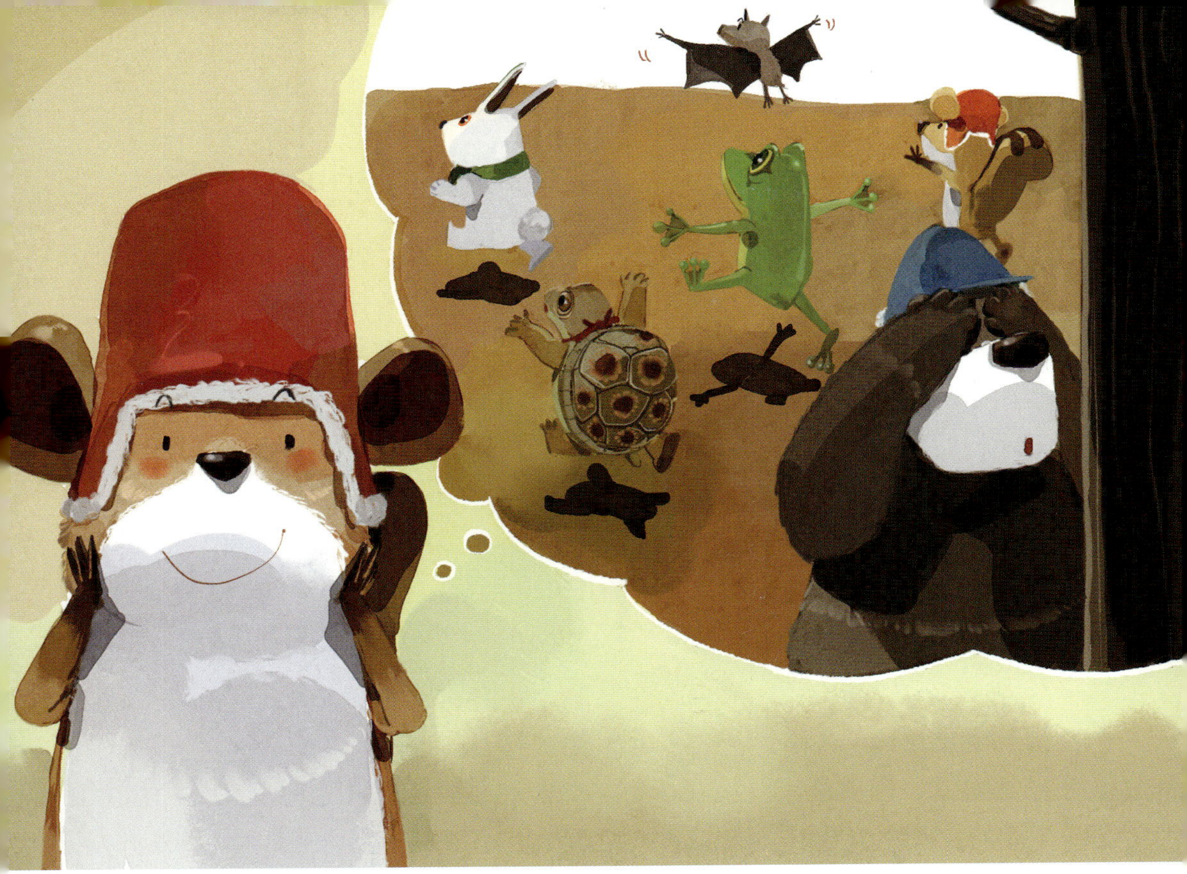

"But I want to play hide-and-seek."

Chip rubbed his paws.

"I want to play with my friends."

Mother shook her head.

"It is not time for hide-and-seek."

POP QUIZ

What game does Chip want to play with his friends?

ⓐ bingo

ⓑ hide-and-seek

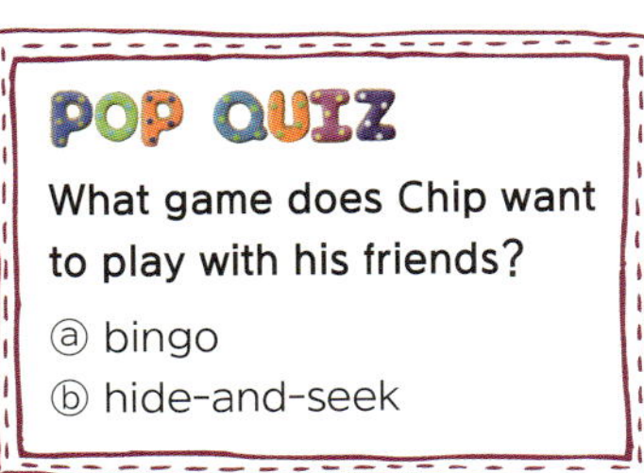

Father said,
"It is time
for hide and
sleep."
"Do we sleep
a long time?"
Chip asked.
"All winter
long."
"We will sleep
until spring," Mother said.
"That is a long nap!" Chip said, surprised.
He did not like naps.

"In winter, there is no food.

So we hibernate," Father said.

"Some animals eat and eat in the fall."

Mother patted her tummy.

"They eat to get fat.

They get fat for the long winter nap."

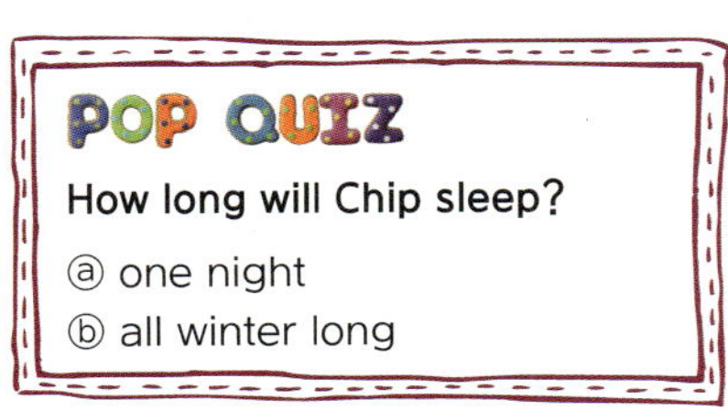

"But we do not get fat," Father said.

"We save nuts and seeds.

We store food in our burrow."

"We may get hungry.

Then we will wake up."

Mother nodded at the nuts.

"We will eat nuts.

We will eat seeds."

"Okay."

Still, Chip did not want to sleep.

"May I play before I sleep?" he asked.

"I want to see my friends."

"First, eat your nuts and seeds."

Mother gave him one more nut.

Chapter One

Comprehension Quiz

A Choose the most similar word in meaning.

❶ hibernate   a) play   b) sleep

❷ store   a) save   b) give

❸ nap   a) sleep   b) hide

B Mark T for true or F for false.

❶ Chip is a hamster.   T F

❷ Chip wants to go to sleep.   T F

❸ The chipmunks will hibernate in the burrow.   T F

❹ The chipmunks eat nuts and seeds.   T F

❺ Chip's family will sleep until spring.   T F

 Choose the best answer to each question.

❶ What does Chip's family store in their burrow?

a) toys

b) twigs

c) food

d) water

❷ What will keep Chip warm while he hibernates?

a) food

b) burrow

c) trees

d) blankets

D Choose the right word for each blank.

❶ Chip's father said, "It is time for hide and ___________."

a) seek

b) play

c) sleep

d) dig

❷ The Chipmunk family will take a long ___________ nap.

a) spring

b) summer

c) fall

d) winter

Chapter Two

Chip Plays Hide-and-Seek

Chip sat on a tree branch.
He ate his nuts and seeds.
The snow began to fall.
Soft and white and cold.

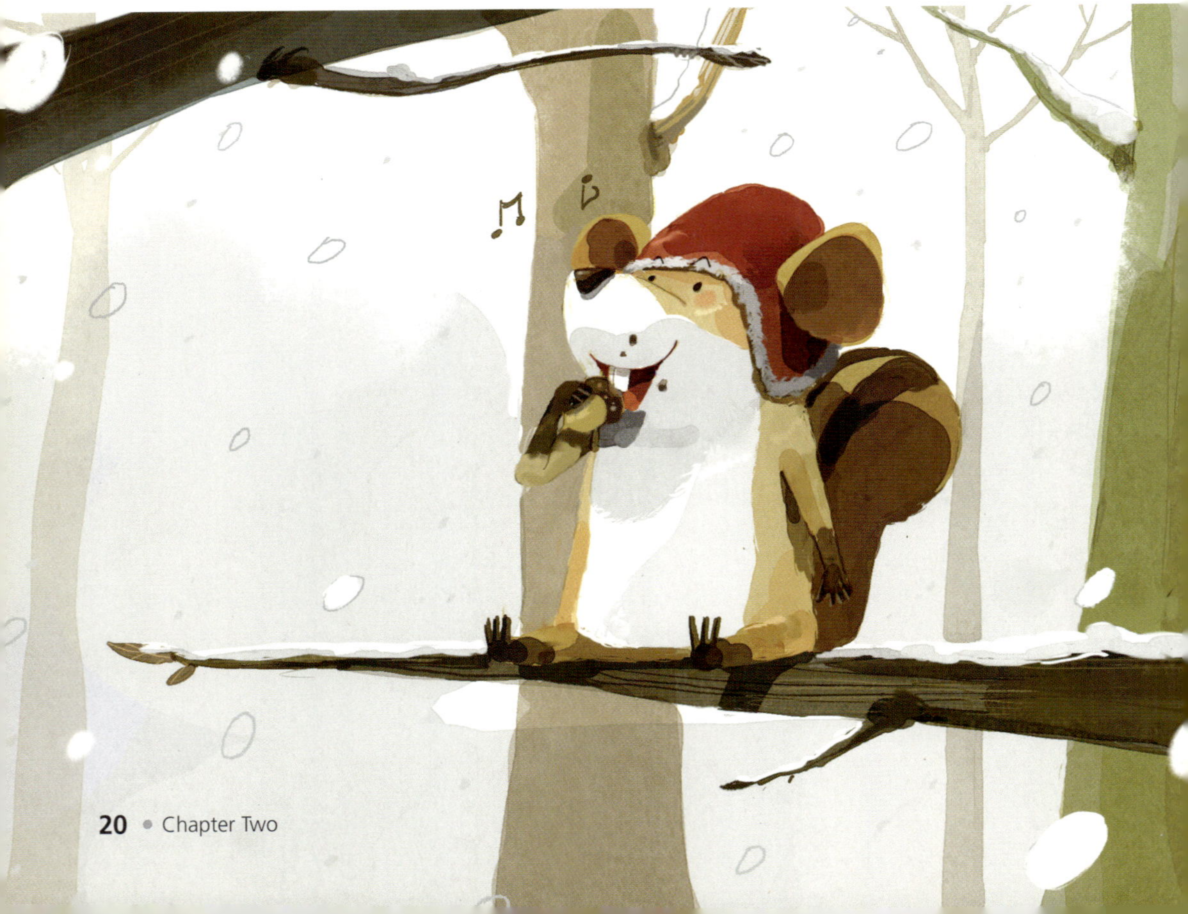

Chip jumped in the trees.

Chip ran on the ground.

He had fun.

He looked for his friends.

"Hello!" he called.

"Black Bear, Black
Bear.

Are you there?"

No one answered.

▲ black bear

KEY WORDS

- **sit on** (sit-sat-sat)
- **begin** (begin-began-begun)
- **fall** (fall-fell-fallen)
- **jump**
- **run** (run-ran-run)
- **on the ground**

- **have fun** (have-had-had)
- **look for**
- **hello**
- **call**
- **no one**

"Green Frog, Green Frog.

Are you under a log?"

He did not hear Green Frog.

He did not see Green Frog.

KEY WORDS

- green frog
- under
- log

- white rabbit
- wait
- little bat

- hear a sound
  (hear-heard-heard)

"White Rabbit, White Rabbit.
Please come out to play. Aha!
Play with me today."
Chip waited.
White Rabbit did not come out to play.
"Little Bat, Little Bat. Where are you at?"
Chip did not hear a sound.

"Why won't my friends play?" Chip asked himself.

"I get it!" Chip flipped his tail.

"You want to play hide-and-seek."

Chip was happy.

Chip liked to play games.

"I will count to ten.

Then I will look for you."

Chip closed his eyes.

He counted.

Chip flipped his tail.

"One," flip.

"Two," flip.

"Three," flip.

"Four, five, six."

Flip, flip, and flip.

"Seven, eight, nine, ten."

Flip, flip, flip, flip went his tail. Aha!

KEY WORDS

- get it
- flip
- tail
- play a game
- ccunt
- close
- go (go-went-gone)

"Ready or not, here I come!"

He opened his eyes.

The ground was white with snow.

He looked for his friends.

He did not see them.

He wiggled his nose.

He did not smell them.

Chip hopped over the snow. Aha!

He sat under a tree. Aha!

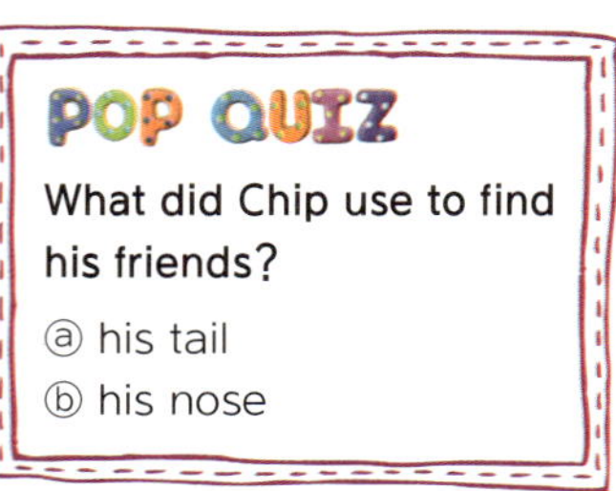

KEY WORDS

- ready or not
- open one's eyes
- wiggle
- smell
- hop
- over the snow

Comprehension Quiz

A Choose all the words that describe snow in the story.

• soft	• happy
• white	• cold
• fun	• little

B Mark T for true or F for false.

1. Chip looks for Black Bear, Green Frog, and White Rabbit. T F
2. Chip is sad. T F
3. Black Bear comes outside to play. T F
4. Chip counts to twenty. T F

 Choose the best answer to each question.

❶ Why did Chip think his friends wanted to play hide-and-seek?

a) They told him they wanted to play.

b) He did not see them so he thought they were hiding.

c) He heard Black Bear count to ten.

d) They told Chip to hide.

❷ What did Chip do as he counted to ten?

a) He wiggled his nose.

b) He opened his eyes.

c) He flipped his tail.

d) He tapped his paw.

D Put the sentences in order.

❶ Chip ate his nuts and seeds.

❷ Chip opened his eyes.

❸ Chip counted to ten.

❹ Chip sat under a tree.

________ → ________ → ________ → ________

Chapter Three

Who Hides under the Ground?

He saw a pile of twigs.
It was under a big tree.
"Is someone hiding under the twigs?"
Chip pushed the twigs away.
He found a small hole.
He went inside.
It was a bear den.
Black Bear was in his den.

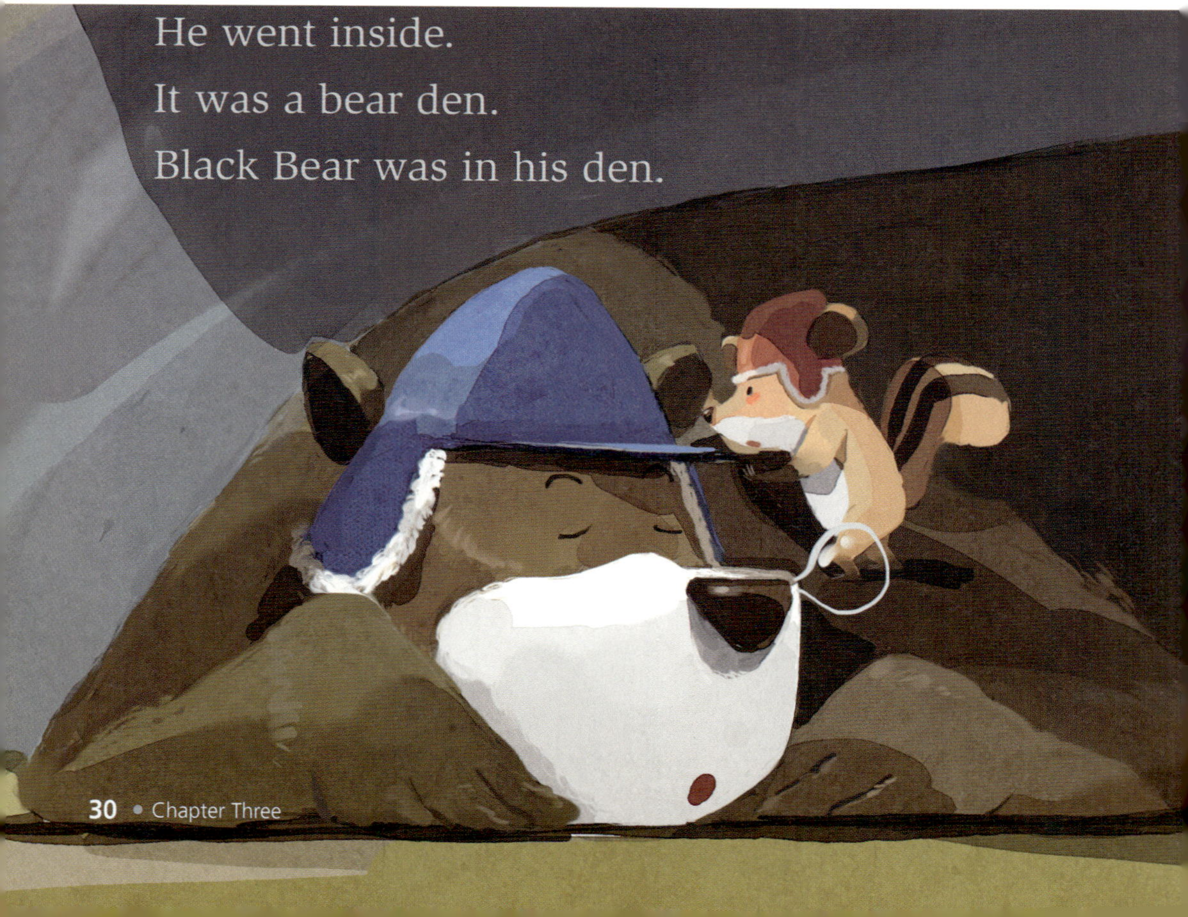

The Black Bear family was sleeping.

Chip jumped on Black Bear.

"Wake up, Black Bear," he said into his ear.

"I found you!"

Black Bear did not move.

His breathing was very slow.

His heartbeat was very slow.

KEY WORDS

- a pile of
- twig
- push away
- find
  (find-found-found)
- hole
- inside
- den
- move
- breathing
- slow
- heartbeat

"Oh, you are hibernating." Aha!

Chip rubbed his paws.

"That is why you ate so many berries," Chip said.

"You were getting fat for the winter."

Chip patted Black Bear on the head.

"Have a nice winter nap.

See you in the spring."

Black Bear did not wake up.

Chip went outside.

He pushed the twigs over the hole.

The twigs hid the Black Bear family den.

KEY WORDS

- that is why
- berry
- pat ~ on the head
- Have a nice winter nap.
- hill
- loose

Chip looked for White Rabbit.

He saw a small hill.

He found some loose grass on the hill.

He pushed the grass away.

He saw a hole.

It was the White Rabbit family burrow.

Chip went inside.

White Rabbit was in the burrow.

All of the White Rabbit family was there.

All the rabbits breathed very slowly.

Their hearts beat very slowly.

Chip touched his friend.

White Rabbit did not move.

KEY WORDS

- all of the
- breathe
- slowly
- beat (beat–beat–beaten)
- touch
- put (put–put–put)
- make a sound (make–made–made)

"White Rabbit, are you hibernating, too?"

White Rabbit did not make a sound.

His nose did not even wiggle.

"Sleep well, White Rabbit," Chip said.

Chip went outside.

He put grass over the burrow.

POP QUIZ

Mark T for true or F for false.

White Rabbit made a sound. T / F

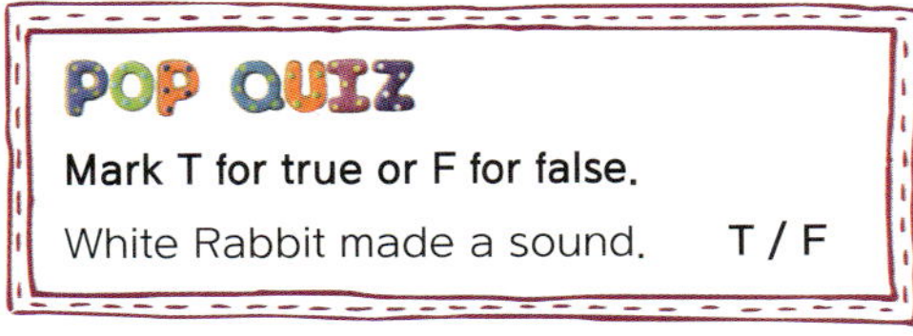

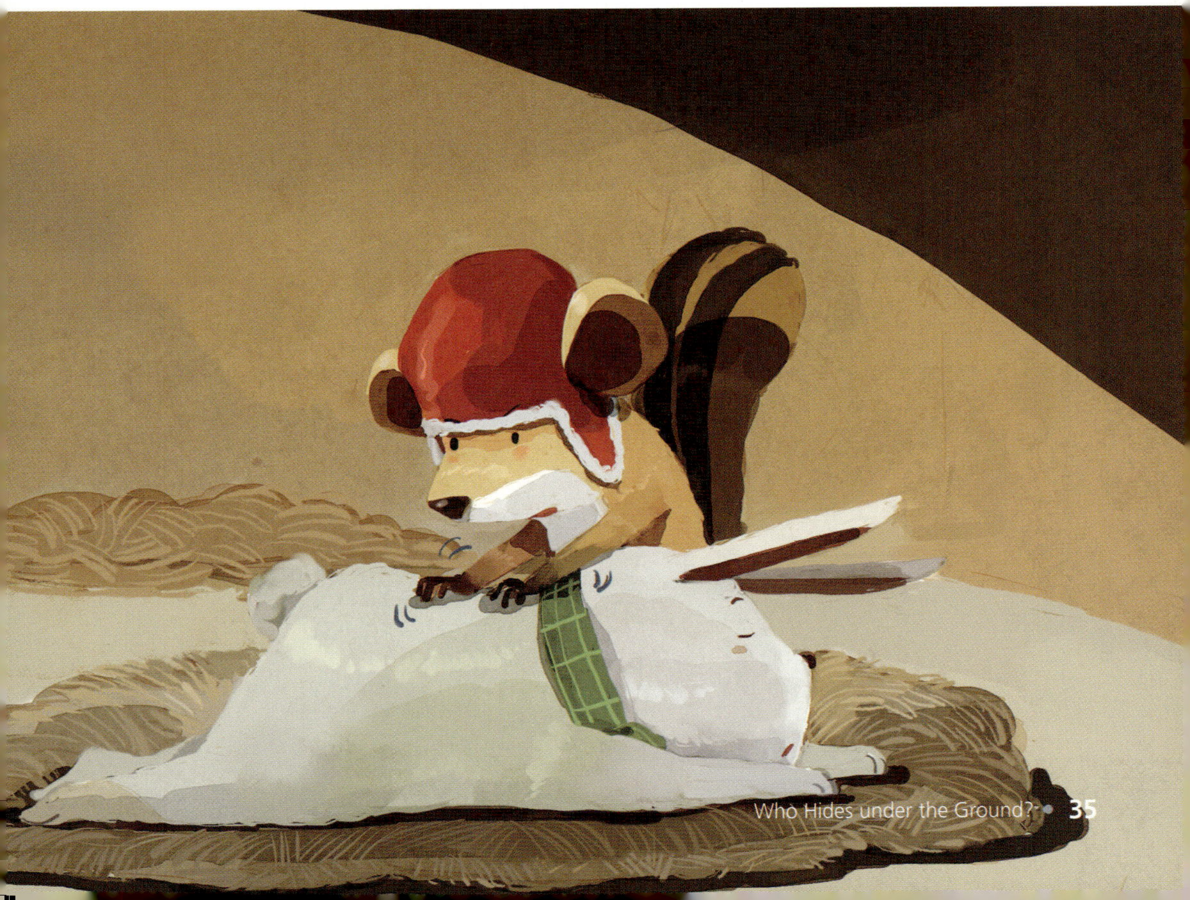

Comprehension Quiz

A Solve the crossword puzzle with the right word in each blank.

Across

❷ White Rabbit sleeps in the ___________.

❹ Black Bear sleeps in his ___________.

Down

❶ ___________ means a long winter nap.

❸ Animals sleeps all the ___________.

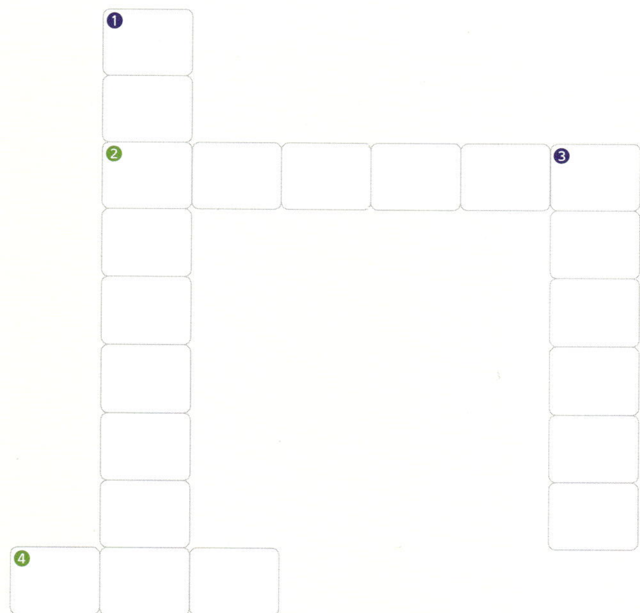

 Choose the best answer to each question.

❶ Why did Chip say Black Bear ate so many berries?

a) He was hungry.

b) He was getting fat for the winter.

c) He liked berries.

d) His mother gave him many berries.

❷ What hid the Black Bear family den?

a) twigs

b) rocks

c) leaves

d) grass

❸ Which is NOT true about White Rabbit?

a) He did not make a sound.

b) His heart beat slow.

c) He did not wiggle his nose.

d) He opened his eyes.

Chapter Four

Who Hides in the Mud?

Chip went to the bank of the river.
He heard, “Ribbit! Ribbit!”
He saw Green Frog digging a hole.
“I see you!” Chip called.
“I see you in the mud!”

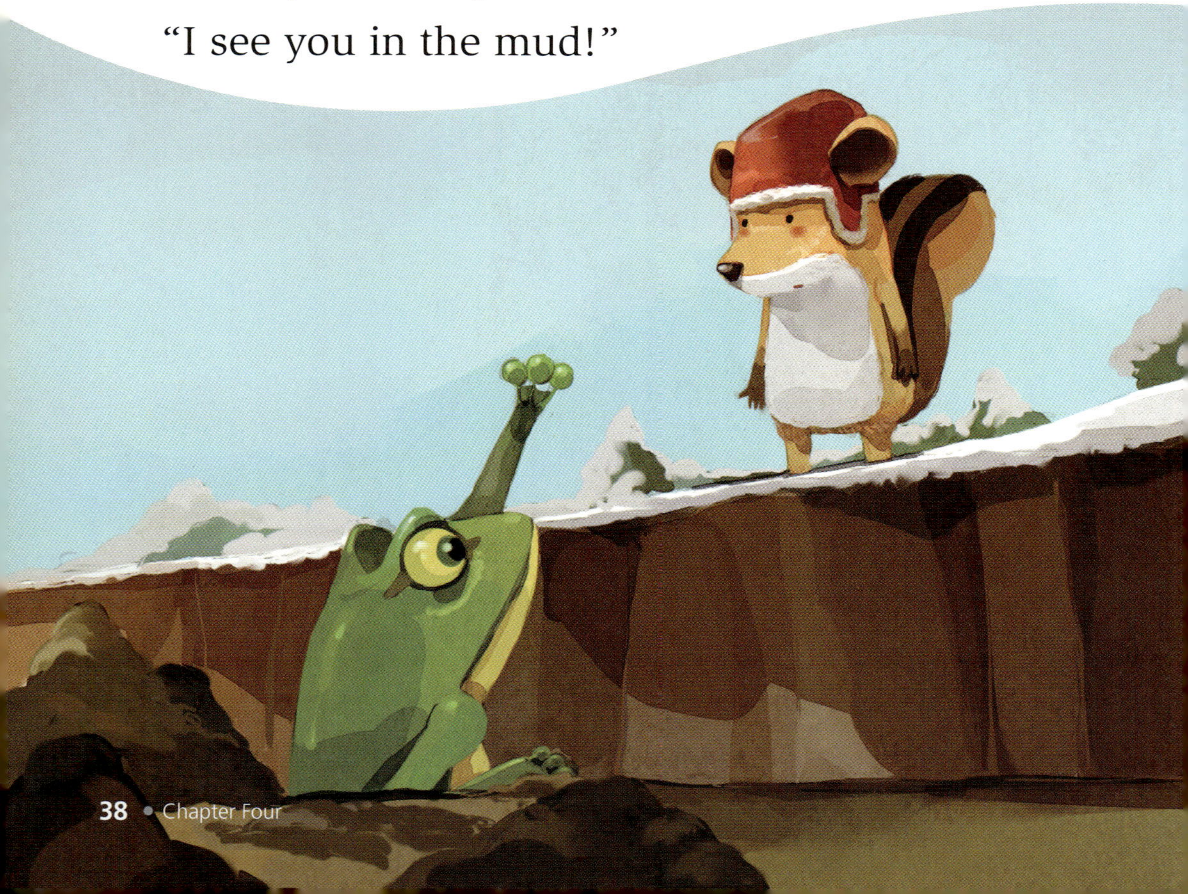

Green Frog said, "Sorry, Chip.

I cannot play hide-and-seek.

I am going to hide and sleep.

I am getting ready to hibernate."

"Do you hibernate in the wet mud?" Chip

asked.

"Yes," Green Frog said.

"I hide deep in the wet mud."

"How do you get air?" Chip asked.

"There is air in the mud.

The mud keeps me warm.

I sleep in the mud."

KEY WORDS

- mud
- bank
- river
- ribbit
- dig (dig-dug-dug)
- be going to
- get ready to
- wet (↔ dry)
- deep
- air

Chip flipped his tail at a dead tree. "Why not hibernate under that log?"

"Slip the Snake is under the log. He will hibernate there."

Green Frog dug in the mud.

"You cannot hibernate with Slip the Snake," Chip shook his head.

"No. Snakes eat frogs and chipmunks," Green Frog said.

"I will not sleep with snakes."

KEY WORDS

- dead
- Why not ~?
- slip
- box turtle

Chip flipped his tail.

He saw Box Turtle walking.

"Box Turtle! 

Do you want to play?"

"No, Chip. It is cold.

It is time to sleep."

▲ box turtle

"Where do you sleep?" Chip asked.

"Do you sleep in your shell?"

"Yes, I do. But I dig in the mud.

I sleep in the mud."

Chip hopped to Box Turtle.

"So you hibernate like Green Frog."

"Yes, I do.

Now I must go to sleep."

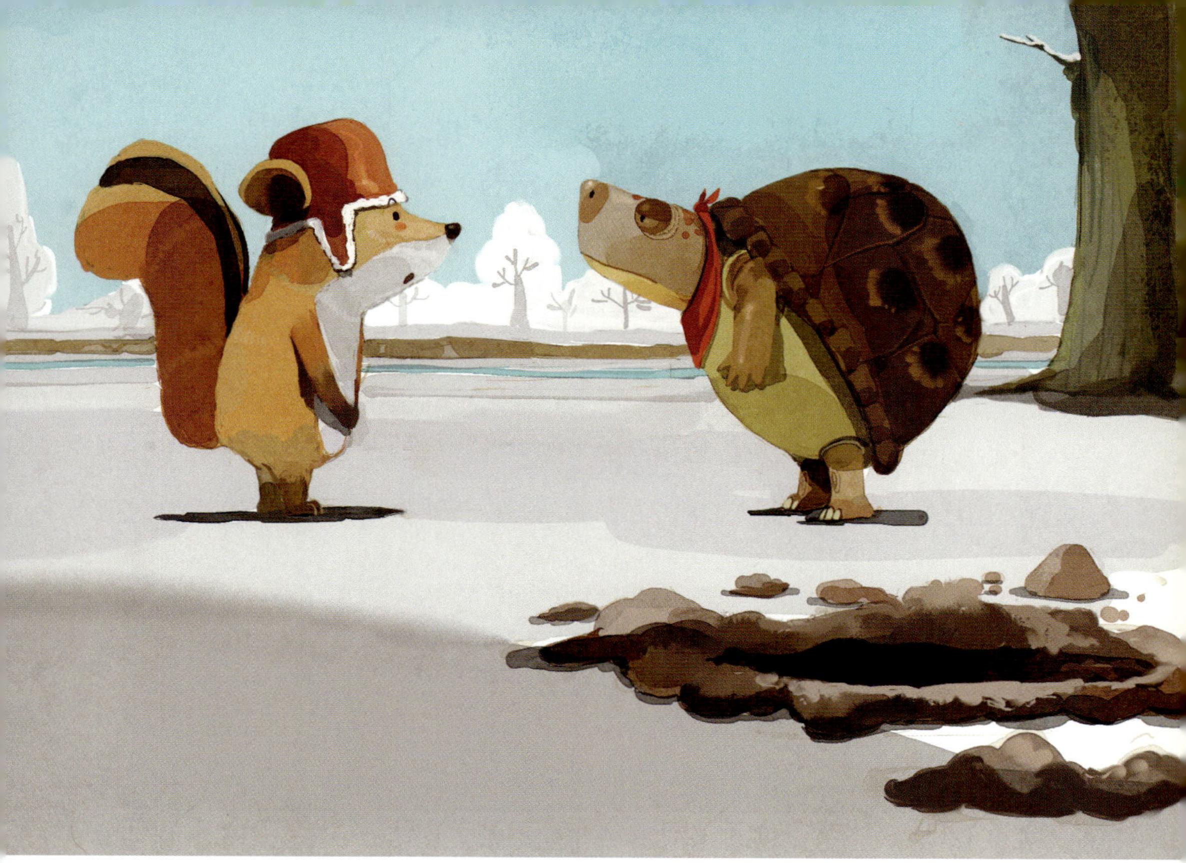

He went into a hole in the mud.

Chip waved goodbye.

"Have a nice winter nap."

Chip hopped away to look for more friends.

POP QUIZ

Where does Box Turtle hibernate?

ⓐ in a log

ⓑ in the mud

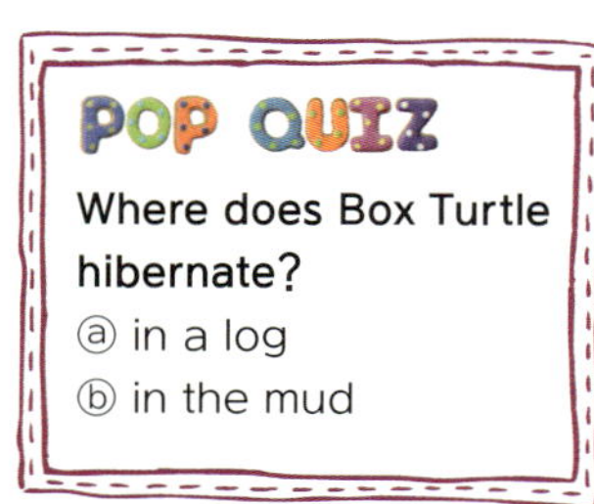

KEY WORDS

- shell
- go to sleep
- wave goodbye

Comprehension Quiz

A Who said what? Match each line with the right animal.

❶ 

a) "Ribbit! Ribbit! I sleep in the mud."

❷ 

b) "I see you in the mud!"

❸ 

c) "I hibernate like Green Frog."

B Mark T for true or F for false.

❶ Green Frog will sleep with a snake.　　T　F

❷ There is air in the mud.　　T　F

❸ Box Turtle will sleep near Green Frog.　　T　F

❹ Slip the Snake will hibernate in the mud.　　T　F

C Choose the right word for each blank.

❶ Slip the Snake was under the ______________.

a) cloud   b) log

c) hole   d) rock

❷ The ______________ keeps Green Frog warm.

a) nuts   b) twigs

c) mud   d) grass

D Choose the best answer to each question.

❶ Choose all the animals that hibernate.

a) Red Fox

b) Black Bear

c) Green Frog

d) Slip the Snake

❷ Which is NOT true?

a) Chip heard "Ribbit, ribbit!" at the bank of the river.

b) Green Frog said, "I can play hide-and-seek."

c) Snakes eat frogs and chipmunks.

d) Chip saw Box Turtle walking.

Chapter Five

Who Sleeps in a Cave?

Chip looked for Little Bat. 

Chip saw a cave.

It was under a big rock.

He looked in the cave.

It was dark inside.

Chip did not see bats on the ground.

He looked at the top of the cave.

He saw black bats.

The black bats hung upside down.

▲ bat

KEY WORDS

- cave
- bat
- dark
- at the top of
- **hang** (hang-hung-hung)
- upside down

They held their wings around their bodies.

Their wings looked like blankets.

"Hello!" Chip called.

No one moved.

Chip saw Little Bat in the cave.

Little Bat was very still.

"All the bats are hibernating, too," Chip said.

"That's why Little Bat ate so many insects."

KEY WORDS

- **hold** (hold-held-held)
- look like
- blanket
- insect

Chip went outside.

Now the snow was deeper.

Big, fat snowflakes fell from the sky.

He saw Red Fox next to a tree. 

Red Fox was looking for food.

Red Fox saw Chip.

Red Fox smiled.

He had big teeth.

Chip flipped his tail.

Red Fox ran to Chip.

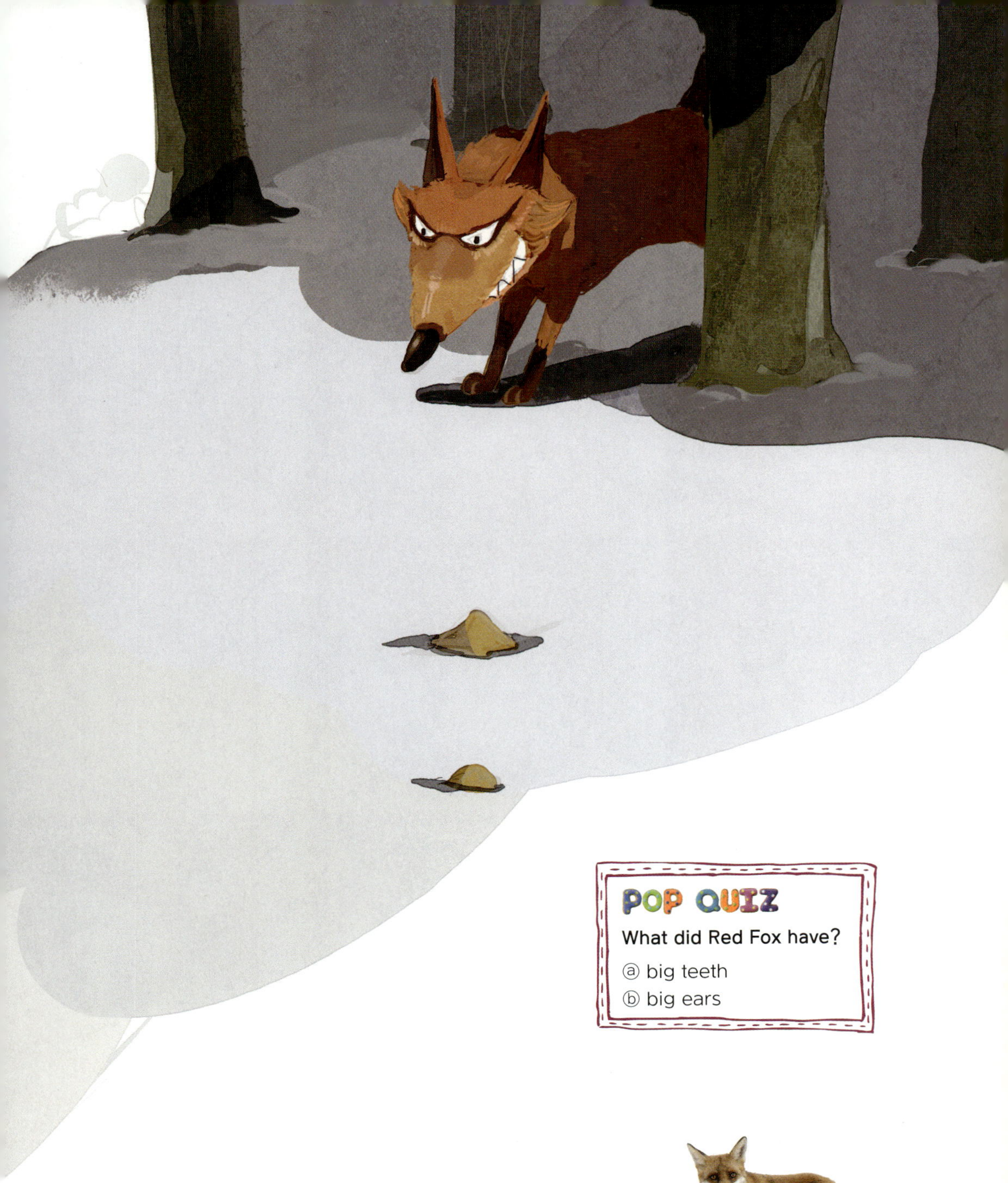

POP QUIZ

What did Red Fox have?

ⓐ big teeth
ⓑ big ears

▲ red fox

KEY WORDS

- deeper
- fat
- snowflake
- next to
- smile
- teeth

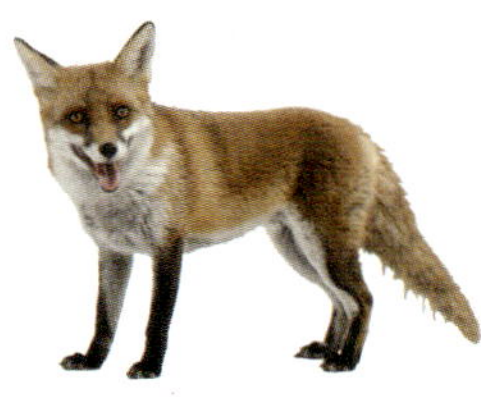

Chip hopped up a tree.

Red Fox sat in the snow.

"Chip, you are too high.

Come down from the tree."

"No, Red Fox, no!

You will not hurt me."

"I will not hurt you."

Red Fox licked his lips.

"Come and play."

"You will not get me.

I will hide."

Chip went into a hole in the tree.

Red Fox gave up.

Red Fox went away.

KEY WORDS

- high
- come down from (come-came-come)
- hurt (hurt-hurt-hurt)
- lick one's lips
- give up
- go away

Comprehension Quiz

A Who said what? Match each line with the right animal.

 ❶  

- a) "Come and play."

- b) "I will hide."

 ❷ 

- c) "All the bats are hibernating."

- d) "Come down from the tree."

B  Mark T for true or F for false.

❶ Bats hibernate in a tree.   T F

❷ It was dark inside the cave.   T F

❸ Chip hid from Red Fox in a tree.   T F

❹ Red Fox did not go away.   T F

C Choose the best answer to each question.

❶ Why did Chip NOT see the bats on the ground?

a) There were no bats in the cave.

b) The bats were playing hide-and-seek.

c) The bats were at the top of the cave.

d) The bats were in a tree.

❷ What was Red Fox doing before he saw Chip?

a) He was looking for food.

b) He was looking for a lost friend.

c) He was looking for his mother.

d) He was looking for his father.

D Put the sentences in order.

❶ Red Fox smiled.

❷ Chip saw Little Bat in the cave.

❸ Chip hopped up a tree.

❹ Red Fox sat in the snow.

_______ → ______ → ______ → ______

Chip Goes Home

"Chip, Chip, Chip!" Mother called.

Chip ran to Mother and Father.

"Red Fox tried to eat me," Chip said.

"It is time to get inside," Father said.

"We must hide from Red Fox."

Mother rubbed her paws.

"The snow is falling.

Soon it will be cold."

KEY WORDS

- try to + *Verb*
- get inside
- soon

- too ~ to...
- stay

Chip went inside the warm burrow.

He sat in the nest of dry grass and leaves.

"It is time to hibernate," Mother said.

"Tell me again.

Why do we have to hibernate?"

"We hibernate in the winter.

It is too cold to stay outside," Mother said. 

"There is no food to gather.

We hibernate to save our energy," Father said.

"And to hide from Red Fox!" Chip said.

"That is right."

Father sat down on the grass nest.

Mother rubbed her paws on her face.

"You will see.

Soon you will be sleepy."

Chip yawned.

He rubbed his eyes.

He blinked.

He did not want to sleep.

He still wanted to play.

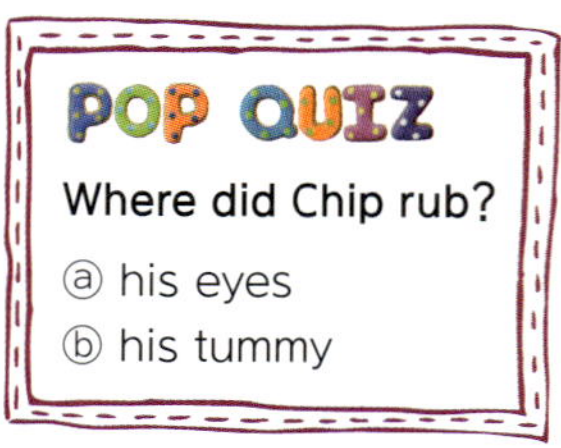

KEY WORDS

- gather
- sit down
- sleepy
- yawn
- blink
- get hungry

"What if I get hungry?" Aha!
Chip patted his tummy.
"Winter is a long time."
"You will not be hungry.
You ate many nuts and seeds," said Mother.

"Your body slows down when you hibernate," said Father.

"So I will not be hungry?"

Chip flipped the tip of his tail.

"There are nuts in our burrow," said Mother.

"If you wake up, you may eat."

Chip yawned again.

He rubbed his eyes.

He rubbed his face.

He rubbed his fur.

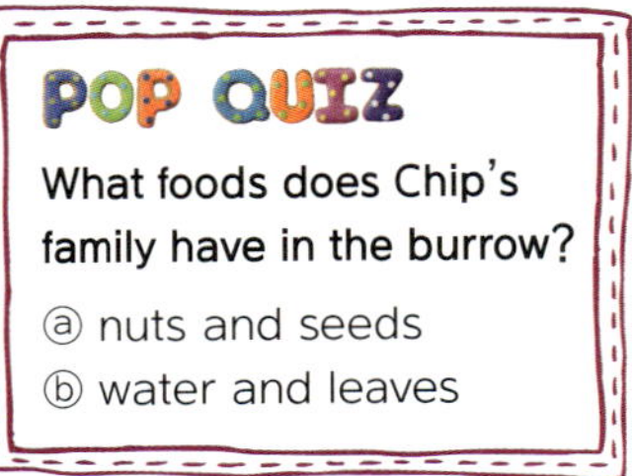

KEY WORDS

▪ slow down   ▪ tip   ▪ fur   ▪ curl up

He was very sleepy.

"Close your eyes, little Chip," Mother said.

"It's time to hide and sleep."

Chip curled up in a nest of leaves.

He closed his eyes.

His breathing slowed down.

His heartbeat slowed down.

He went to sleep for his long winter nap.

Mother and Father curled up next to Chip.

"See you in the spring," Mother said.

Outside, the snow fell.

Thick, fat snowflakes filled the sky.

Soon the ground had a deep, thick blanket of snow.

The whole world was white.

All the animals were inside.

Bears were in dens.

Frogs and turtles were in the mud.

Snakes were under logs.

Bats were in caves.

Rabbits were in burrows.

Chip was snug and warm with Mother and Father.

Everything was quiet.

Everyone went to hide and sleep.

Comprehension Quiz

A Choose all the expressions that describe the season and outdoor scenes in the story.

• no food to gather	• fat snowflakes
• time for hide-and-seek	• upside down
• too cold to stay outside	• cold and green

B Fill in each blank with the right word below.

hide	sleepy	energy	slow

❶ Animals hibernate to save _________________.

❷ Chip's father said, "We must _________________ from Red Fox."

❸ Chip's breathing ______________ed down.

❹ Chip was very ______________.

C Choose the best answer to each question.

❶ What three things did Chip do when he was sleepy?

a) He rubbed his eyes.

b) He rubbed his face.

c) He ran out of the burrow.

d) He yawned.

❷ Where did Chip curl up?

a) in a nest of warm fur

b) in a nest of grass and leaves

c) in a nest of nuts and seeds

d) in a nest of twigs

D Mark T for true or F for false.

❶ In the winter, there is no food to gather. T F

❷ When Chip hibernates, his heartbeat slows down. T F

❸ Chip is snug and warm in the burrow. T F

❹ Rabbits and chipmunks both sleep in burrows. T F

Let's Review the Story

Fill in the blanks to review the story.

❶ **Title:** ________________

❷ **Main Characters:** __________, Mother, Father

❸ **Detail 1:** Hibernate means to __________ all winter.

   Detail 2: Animals hibernate when there is no __________.

   Detail 3: Animals hibernate in dens, burrows, m__________,

and c__________.

❹ **Summary:**
- It was winter. Chip wanted to __________ with his friends. He did not want to __________.
- Chip went to see Black Bear. He was hibernating in his __________.
- Chip went to see White Rabbit. He was hibernating in his __________.
- Chip went to see Green Frog. He was getting ready to hibernate.
- Green Frog and Box Turtle will hibernate in the __________.
- Red Fox was looking for food. Red Fox wanted to __________ Chip.
- Chip ran to his b__________. Chip went to sleep for a long winter n__________.

Let's Think & Talk

Think about the following questions and answer them freely.

❶ Did you know about "hibernation" before you read the book? Or did you learn about it for the first time? Tell us what you thought when you first heard about hibernation and what you have learned about it.

❷ Different animals hibernate in different places. Imagine you could be one of the animals in the book. What animal would you be and where would you go to have a winter sleep?

❸ If animals didn't hibernate, what do you think would happen?

Let's Review the Story

❶ Title: Hide and Sleep

❷ Main Characters: Chip, Mother, Father

❸ Detail 1: Hibernate means to sleep all winter.

Detail 2: Animals hibernate when there is no food.

Detail 3: Animals hibernate in dens, burrows, mud, and caves.

❹ Summary:
- It was winter. Chip wanted to play with his friends. He did not want to sleep.
- Chip went to see Black Bear. He was hibernating in his den.
- Chip went to see White Rabbit. He was hibernating in his burrow.
- Chip went to see Green Frog. He was getting ready to hibernate.
- Green Frog and Box Turtle will hibernate in the mud.
- Red Fox was looking for food. Red Fox wanted to eat Chip.
- Chip ran to his burrow. Chip went to sleep for a long winter nap.

- Hide and Sleep
- Level 1
- 16 Questions

(Vocabulary 5 / Reading Comprehension 10 /

Sentence Structure & Grammar 1)

1. What does "hibernate" mean?
   ① to sleep all winter
   ② to play in the snow
   ③ to play hide-and-seek
   ④ to sleep all summer

2. Choose the best word for the blank.

   A burrow means a(n) "______________" in the ground.

   ① nap
   ② tail
   ③ cage
   ④ home

3. Which word is most similar to "flip"?
   ① turn
   ② run
   ③ sit
   ④ stand

4. Choose the pair of words that are opposites.
   ① sleep ↔ close
   ② full ↔ hungry
   ③ warm ↔ quiet
   ④ dark ↔ snug

5. What does Green Frog say?

① ribbit

② woof

③ chip

④ roar

6. Where did Chip see the loose grass?

① on the river bank

② under a big rock

③ on a small hill

④ inside the Black Bear family den

7. Where does Box Turtle hibernate?

① in the cave

② in the log

③ in the burrow

④ in the mud

8. What is NOT a reason that animals hibernate?

① There is no food to gather.

② It's too cold to stay outside.

③ The animals should save their energy.

④ The animals should stay inside and eat all winter long.

9. What happens while animals hibernate?

① Heartbeats of the animals slow down.

② All the animals never wake up.

③ Animals breathe fast.

④ Some animals often go outside to get some air.

※ Choose the right word for each blank. (10~13)

10.

The bats' wings looked like _______________.

① rocks
② logs
③ snow
④ blankets

11.

Chip's father said, "We must _______________ from Red Fox."

① run
② hide
③ jump
④ hop

12.

"Eat your food, Chip. Then we must _______________ all winter."

① sleep
② play
③ gather
④ store

13.

Chip sat in the nest of dry _______________ and _______________.

① grass, leaves
② leaves, mud
③ seeds, nuts
④ grass, mud

※ **Choose the common word for the two blanks. (14~15)**

14.

- "Wake up, Black Bear," Chip said into Black Bear's ear.
  Black Bear ________________.
- Chip touched White Rabbit.
  White Rabbit ________________.

① cried loudly
② woke up
③ did not move
④ did not feel well

15.

Some animals eat and eat in the fall. They eat to get ____________.
They get ____________ for the long winter nap.

① sleepy
② hungry
③ warm
④ fat

16. What is the wrong part?

It is <u>to</u> <u>cold</u> <u>to</u> <u>stay</u> <u>outside</u>.
   ① ② ③   ④

Suzanne Pitner

Suzanne Pitner is a teacher and writer who has enjoyed visiting Alaska, exploring Rome, teaching in China, and is looking forward to more world travel. She has a Master's Degree in Education, and is a graduate of the Long Ridge Writer's Group. In addition to writing educational articles and books, she writes historical fiction and contemporary fiction for young adults using the pen name Suzanne Lilly.

Hide and Sleep

Written by Suzanne Pitner
Illustrated by Yu Kang Kim

First Published in December 2014
Second Printing in June 2018

Editorial Manager: Juyon Choi
Editors: Juyon Choi, Kyunghee Jang, Jiyeong Park
Designer: Eunhee Lee
Cover Designer: Eunhee Lee

Published and distributed by

Happy House

Darakwon Bldg., 64-1 Jandari-ro, Mapo-gu, Seoul, Korea 04031
Tel: 82-2-736-2031(ext. 250)   Fax: 82-2-732-2037
Homepage: www.ihappyhouse.co.kr
Publisher: Kyudo Chung

ISBN: 978-89-6653-157-8 18740 / 978-89-6653-156-1 18740(set)

[Components]
• 1 Audio CD (Recording Studio: Aram)
• Answer Keys & Korean Translation: Free download at www.ihappyhouse.co.kr